SOCIAL MEDIA MARKETING MASTERY 2021

How to Win on the Web and Make Money Online with Facebook, Instagram, YouTube, Twitter, LinkedIn and Pinterest

Oliver Alexander Martin

considered an endorsement from the trademark
holder.

Table of Contents

What is Social Media Marketing ?

Social Media Marketing seems to be the latest word to improve people's visibility and sales online, but social media is it all cracked?

Social Media Marketing businesses are now coming up everywhere these days, and they encourage anyone to listen to how incredibly important social media such as Facebook Twitter and YouTube is to the company but does marketing to social networks actually work for all the hype for the medium-sized and small business?

Is it really worth spending a small fortune on recruiting a Social Media Marketing company?

So did someone actually do their homework on this before someone hired to create a business page on Facebook?

Many Social Media Marketing companies set up business pages for 600 to $1,000 or more like Facebook (which are free) and tell customers they don't need a website, since Facebook is the world's biggest social network, and everybody has a Facebook account.

Now that Facebook is the world's largest social network, and yes, Facebook users are potential customers, does it really matter?

Marketing social media companies are all too eager to show the advantages of social media such as how many tweets and how many users on Twitter or last year were sent and how much people watch videos on YouTube, etc., but do you get the full overview?

Once, he sat next to a Social Media Marketing specialist at a business seminar that spruce everyone who got to hear about the incredible benefits of setting up a small-scale Facebook business page (with him, of course) and selling it on Twitter.

Therefore, intrigued by these "experts"' suggestions, he only looked up on Facebook to see that he had only 11 friends on Facebook (not a good start).

So the study decided to look at Social Media Marketing to know if it worked, for whom it worked, and whether it did, why did social media marketing work for them? And should the company rely so heavily on sales across social networks?

As a web developer, multiple social networking problems were always facing (and increasing), where potential customers said that making a website sounds good, but they had a Facebook business page and that several sources (the unofficial but anonymous one "they") had said Social networks were the thing to do.

Why is the development of a quality website for small and medium-sized businesses still preferred over any type of social network? Okay, it's clear, since social media are social media and social networks aren't business networks or business networks (this is more like LinkedIn).

That sounds simple but real and is backed up by statistics. The argument is that social media marketing doesn't suggest that Facebook is not a social network and despite the fact that Facebook and Google users are the around same number, people don't use Facebook as much as they are using a search engine like Google (which has around half of the search engine market). You use it to establish contact with friends and family or for news and entertainment.

A recent study by the International Business Machines Institute for Business Value reveals that around 55% of all social media users do not engage brands on social media, and only about 23% actively use social media deliberately to communicate with brands. Today, the majority (66 percent) of all people that are using social media and engaging with companies knowingly or not say they need to know that a company interacts sincerely before they connect.

And how do you use ads in social media? And is it worth it?

Okay, first of all, getting a well-optimized website would bring you far more business than social media in the majority of cases, mainly if you are a small to medium-sized local company because far more customers will join a search engine like Google, Yahoo, and Bing as many as they will ever do in social media, and if you do not have a website you are missing Given all the (not that good) numbers, however, it is still a good idea for businesses to use the social media just as many Social Media Marketing professionals do today, why? Because it obviously doesn't work the way they say it does.

Social Media Marketing businesses and business in general considered social networks like Facebook to be fresh opportunities for picking up, and when Facebook started picking up the millions of PayPal co-founder Peter Thiel investing US$ 500,000 for 7% of their company (in June 2004) with a few risk capital firms betting on Facebook and in October 2007, Microsoft annually invested on Facebook. Nevertheless, both Social Media Marketing Companies and Company failed to make good use of the considerable number of Facebook users online since Facebook's humble beginnings to now (2012).

The reality is that quantities don't suit buyers. Is it in the best interest of a social media marketing firm to discuss social networks?

Definitely. Absolutely. Is it best for people in a social network like Facebook to assume that businesses will mass-sell through advertising and marketing for them?

It is, of course. Late in 2012, Facebook announced that its income soared 65 percent to 1 billion dollars in the previous year as its advertising revenue jumped almost 90 percent to 3,71 billion dollars, so the Social Media Marketing model works well for you, but is it working for you?

Yeah, statistically, but that doesn't automatically mean it won't.

There is a significant difference between social networks and search engines.

Those who use Google are willing to look for something, so if they are searching for hairdressers at that moment.

They're looking for something.

The primary intention is generally to connect with friends and family with something like Facebook. Mark Zuckerberg said, "I do not believe that social networks can be monetized as research engines... we need to find out in three years ' time what the ideal model is.

Perception is one of the most significant problems facing businesses with social networks and Social Media Marketing. International Business Machines Institute of Business Value study showing "significant gaps between what businesses believe consumers care and what customers want from their social media interactions with businesses.

" For example, in today's society people will not only give you reviews, Facebook likes, comment or information, but also the old adage The main reason most people connect on social media with brands or companies is to get deals, but brands and businesses themselves believe that the main reason people communicate with them is to learn about new products through social media.

Of firms and companies that offer discounts, their list of why people interact with them is just 12th. Many corporations believe that social media would improve activism, but only 38% of customers agree.

Organizations must find more innovative ways of linking to social media if they plan to see some kind of impact. The International Business Machines research has shown some positive initiatives in businesses that have been able to use social media for their advantages. The study has taken into account the fact that customers list "good discounts or coupons" and "customer products and services" as the top two activities when they are asked what they do when engaging with organizations or brands through social media. There is also a fantastic Twelpforce initiative introduced by Best Buys in the U.S., where employees can answer questions about their customers via Twitter. The profit with both

Twelpforce and Cold Stone Creamery is simply for the customer which are potential. Sadly, the big trick of social media marketing is to sell the majority of social media marketing without trying to sell (or looking like your selling).

Creating a meaningful user connection via social media is not easy and perhaps most useful for businesses to use social media to boost their Google rankings on their websites. Yet the company must understand that you can't just build a business page on Facebook and hope for the best. Social Media Marketing requires commitment, and potential customers need to see the value for what they are offering through their social media activities, and then you can achieve better results.

Social Media Marketing Mistakes

Imagine this.

You purchase some products online, and it takes far longer than it should arrive. Additionally, there are a few things missing in the box. Frustrated, you go to the Facebook page of the seller to voice your complaints and expect compensation.

Yet, in spite of persistent prodding, radio silence at the other end is complete.

Didn't the experience feel good?

You think this business might not care about you-how you relied on it to provide you with a good experience, and instead, it destroyed this trust. So you do what any disappointed person does-you never pledge to buy from here again and press the "unlike" button.

There's a lesson to be learned here for social media strategists. A plan for social media marketing will inevitably twist with a few unlike and contrary comments.

Social media, as a business owner, gives you a limited opportunity to make a good impression. Whether you take advantage of these opportunities will make or break your business.

The evidence is found in:

- 71% of users who encounter positive social interaction with a brand possibly suggest it-ambassador
- According to a survey, almost 20% of social media posts do not replicate the emotional effect on social media
- 42% of Twitter users expect a company to address their inquiries in an hour.

Here are a few mistakes which you could have ignored:

Be reckless with negative feedback.

If you've ever worked with a dealer, you won't expect him to stand up for him when you have a question or carelessly.

So why would your social media followers?

Keep in mind that when someone asks you something derogatory on social media, the majority of your followers can see it. And they're as interested in seeing how you react.

This is a nail-biting case for corporations. But it can be avoided entirely.

Put a competent person behind the wheel: experienced professionals as social media experts should take an impartial approach to criticism and realize that it does not serve any purpose if they are reckless.

For starters, they know that it doesn't really benefit anybody to respond to comments like "your service sucks. I want my money back." A well-formulated reaction improves both your credibility and the rising temperament.

In order to explain, the response should be something like, "We are sorry that you've had a bad experience. Can you tell us exactly what happened to us so that we can make changes?"

Get warning by using online tools: something you don't see every day is easy to forget. The social media comments are the same. You can't track them all. Nobody inboxes you, and no promise exists that followers can sign you.

You can use software such as Google Alerts to monitor all comments when people use their keywords in your social media fields.

Use tools for managing social media to schedule the same posts on all platforms.

Management of Social media tools let marketers to publish the content of same simultaneously on social media several platforms. Most organizations use it for planning posts. And it worked for them too, giving them time to focus on other things.

Yet, people often use these methods to prepare the same contents on most platforms. This is tactic lazy and let know that it doesn't matter how viewers interpret the content.

Keep in mind that on LinkedIn, what works on Facebook or Twitter won't always work. With different target audiences in mind, through social media platform was created. For instance, a 140-character tweet isn't going to sit well with LinkedIn audiences expecting broader posts.

Using software to schedule customized publications. First, develop the social media strategy and make the most of social sharing resources. Take the time to learn about each platform's unique capabilities. If it takes, limit yourself to two or three platforms. For example, image-rich posts on Google+ are more effective.

HubSpot and Hootsuite are two of the many apps you can use to organize posts and even see which channels play the most. Such platforms offer free online social marketing courses, as well as automated information sharing, which can allow you to optimize and site by adapting your posts to different social media channels.

3. Skimping on buttons for social sharing.

Corporate owners usually reserve their best website content. For example, content such as insightful blogs establish them as experts in their niches.

It also offers people the opportunity to stay on these websites longer. Maybe they want to look around to see what else is available?

Sadly, you can have content that everyone wants to share-but if the tourists have no way to share it, the visibility that they are searching for won't be available.

Make your social sharing work on mobile devices: Statistics show that more than 15 percent of twitter mentions come from tweets embedded on your platform. This also shows that people share a great deal on mobile devices.

Software to create WordPress Social Sharing Buttons: You can create personalized social sharing buttons for different audiences by using online tools.

When selecting appropriate plug-ins, it is an excellent rule to choose those which allow you to create greater freedom for various platforms in the type of social share buttons.

For instance, you could tell your developers to download WordPress plugin tools such as Easy Share Buttons Adder to create unique sharing keys for your web and mobile audience and add them to any social media posts to increase interaction with mobile audiences.

Add this is another plugin tool.

Getting a social budget: it's worth doing something if anything is worth doing. Tools like Easy Share Button Adder can be downloaded and used free of charge.

But, if you really want to make your sharing buttons shine, you better have a budget for it and use it to buy your pro or premium packages. They offer more flexibility and retail options for about $10 to $100.

Use content that can be shared wisely: if you want to use social media, the content needs to be something people want to share. For example, Image rich posts are much more shared than text-based content.

Find infographics to demonstrate. Studies show that social media infographics are posted and "liked" 3 times more than any other content.

Using software to alert yourself to negative comments and rely on professional assistance. Take the lazy way out by using the car posting technique. Pay attention to the type of content, how your followers share content on your chosen social platforms, and customize it to extend your scope for mobile applications.

It is a mistake to find social approaches to market the brand quickly and easily. Time, energy, and dedication are required. Thinking about mistakes and inconvenience will help you avoid them.

Social Media Marketing Importance

Interaction in the technological world has become simpler than ever. The planet has now decreased from a large population to a network of people living in a global village. People from around the world have gotten closer, and distances have reduced so far that a human is just a click away.

A new theory, the notion of six degrees of separation, has arisen in this ever-growing network of people. The theory behind it is that only six individuals are a chain between you and any other person in the world. It underlines the importance of online communication and the manner in which the environment has been diminished considerably.

This is the influence of social media and of online communication technologies. An occurrence in one part of the world takes a matter of seconds to the second part. Imagine if you were involved in this news or case. The value of this technology is its ease of use. You will benefit from this method in a full number of ways.

Social media marketing takes your name to global prominence.

This is your internationally renowned book. Your business or brand can be identified with millions of followers and fans worldwide.

Millions of people can use these platforms to communicate online and express their opinions. When you join the social media marketing realm, all these people are your prospects.

Your services are just one search away.

As a severe product, support your company or commodity.

This technology gives you access to almost the entire planet and all its inhabitants. You're there to read and discuss anything you need to say. This is your opportunity to create an impression of "Hey! I'm here to do business" and "I'm serious about the products and services I'm delivering."

Make you vulnerable without too much effort to thousands of individuals.

Marketing in social media is virtually free. If you tried to reach millions of people through physical means, you would need to invest a lot. This platform is the best way to reach your potential customers effectively, not only in financial terms but also in terms of time.

Give feedback on the kind of viewer you have.

The degree of input you might receive is an exciting thing about marketing on these social websites. In reality, social media marketing will show you people who are interested in your product or service or are interested in it.

This gives you a better chance to change your strategies and achieve better results.

You will find out how many people visit your page or the ages of people who comment or share your message or even their race, place, religion, hobbies, and preferences.

You inform the world about your product, and social media marketing educates the people who have taken an interest in your company. You get to know them personally via the social media network.

Set up an active communication channel between you and your client.

Your customer may have a question or may need assistance or would like to know more about your product. Your presence in social media allows you to respond to him directly. This, in effect, assures the consumer that you are responsible and trustworthy.

Your company is treated as an individual.

In general, people may not want to do business with a company or organization and prefer working with individuals. Because a person is real, he's in this world, and he's someone you can relate to, he's got feelings, thoughts, and emotions. This gives your company a human personification in social media. It seems to be more a person than a company; someone can speak to somebody who can meet. It provides a comfort zone for your consumers and generates advantages for both.

Render it more available to you.

Social media sites guarantee your attendance 24 hours a day, seven days a week. Your customer can quickly drop a message and respond as soon as you want. It strengthens the bond between you and your client and encourages a sense of loyalty to your brand. This persistent flexibility cannot be seen in the physical office due to the opening and closing hours of the office. This convenience for consumers to reach you when necessary, can only be assured by social media.

Social media are the field of play.

Whether you're a multinational company or a new organization, you're all at the same stage in the world of social media.

Through social media, finances and wealth may not make much of a difference.

The ability to communicate and attract people and the quality of the product or services you provide is what makes a difference.

In the physical world, new start-ups face enormous financial challenges throughout trying to promote themselves while the promotion of giant companies continues. The network of social media provides a fair field to show your true spirit and abilities.

You may discover new customers or potential customers.

You can begin to see clear trends in your business answer when analyzing your reviews from viewers. Customers from a particular region that you never felt you were involved in are your best customers.

Such trends help you to see some unscrewed markets that you can take advantage of.

You can move quickly and take advantage of the opportunity.

Marketing campaigns are easier to manage and more economical.

To build up the campaign for social media marketing needs a lot less work than to physically conduct your marketing campaign, like putting up banners or ads, etc. Marketing in social media is relatively easy to manage and updated quite often.

Your network is rapidly expanding.

With more people adding to your social network, more people will join.

When we continue to add the pace at which people are added, they expand. And your business would do like the tree branches down.

Social media is more open to men.

People tend to pay more attention to social media stuff.

This is because people believe that there is no political agenda behind facts or the involvement of large companies trying to sell their products compared with traditional marketing social media. We are the only people who share their expertise and opinions.

Therefore, social media posts tend to be paid more attention and are affected more by them than professional content.

People check their social media news daily for posts made by friends and family, and there you are with your latest news or promotion between all their messages.

The readers will pay attention to what they have been trying to communicate and then forward the news to their friends, and the word will spread exponentially.

The current generation of information and communication sharing is social media. Almost everybody keeps their presence clear online.

You should not remain behind the competition and take advantage of this technology.

The research presented preliminary evidence in order to answer this question.

With a national survey, we analyzed how much it is used daily and how emotionally engaged people are with the sites with three health-related results: social well-being, positive mental wellbeing, and self-rated fitness.

We found, for example, that daily social media is used by social media as part of everyday life in response to content posted by others that is positively related to all three health outcomes.

Emotional interactions with social media, for example, are negatively correlated with all three outcomes if apps are reviewed for fear of missing out, deceit, and isolated from friends when not logging in to social media.

More generally, these findings suggest that daily usage alone cannot be a concern, as long as we are conscientious users. In addition, it could be beneficial.

Behavioral interventions can help people with inappropriate social media usage. For example, programs that build "effortful control" capabilities that allow behavioral self-regulation has proven to be useful in the problem of the Internet and social media.

We are used to hearing that the use of social media is detrimental to mental health and well-being, especially for young people. Did you find it interesting that it could have positive effects?

The findings run counter to what some would predict, which is unusual. We recognize that a strong social network has positive mental health and well-being. Routine use of social media can account for reduced face to face social interactions in busy lives. Social media can provide people with a forum to transcend distance and time barriers, encourage them to communicate and reconnect with others, extend and improve them in personal networks and interactions. Yes, this is confirmed by some empirical evidence.

And On the other hand, increasing research has shown that the use of social media is negatively associated with mental health and wellbeing and can lead to increased risk of depression and anxiety, for example, among young people.

The book suggests that the approaches that individuals use social media may have a more significant impact than the frequency and duration of use on their mental health and wellbeing.

INTRODUCTION
SOCIAL MEDIA MARKETING
VS DIGITAL MARKETING

Social media marketing is often regarded as equivalent to **digital marketing**, so that sometimes the two phrases are used as synonyms.

In truth, social media marketing is **only a part** of digital marketing.

As a matter of fact, those who decide to invest in digital marketing, develop more complex strategies which include diversified investments (for example, in search marketing and **email marketing**) and – why not – aim for more traditional media such as radio and TV as profitable asset.

Digital marketing uses all digital channels to promote the product or the **brand**, while social media marketing works only with social platforms.

SOCIAL MEDIA MARKETING VS SOCIAL MEDIA ADVERTISING

For a better understanding of aims and objectives, we need to make another important distinction: social media marketing **is not**, and not only, **social media advertising**.

Social media advertising refers only to paid strategies: over the years most social platforms have developed **paid services** (such as **Facebook Ads**) which allow marketer and other people involved in business to modulate investments and set up campaigns aiming to reach their core target, improve conversions, succeed in lead generation and so on.

Social media marketing (SMM) lives on much more than **sponsored contents**: its "mission" is to **enhance the digital presence** of the brand or the product in connection with its **visibility** and

positioning and, in a long chain reaction, also with the **purchase decisions** of the end user.

FACTORS TO CONSIDER FOR A GOOD SOCIAL MEDIA MARKETING PLAN

It's easy to understand that, like any other traditional marketing strategy, a social media marketing strategy can't be improvised. You have to consider **several factors**:

- First of all, your **goals**, both the short-term and the long-term ones. For example, a new **brand** launched on an unexplored market or even a well-known brand which has started a **brand extension** process, may need to improve their **brand awareness**. A social media marketing campaign can be the ideal solution if you want to build hype for a new product launch, while the feedbacks from your community could be useful, with a preventive function, for a **rebranding** process. In addition, a lot of people coming from different environments have used social media to deliver **customer** service or to solve, at least from a communicative point of view, company crises.

- Your **target audience**. The myth that social media are used only by young people should be really debunked. According to the data from Statista, an online statistics portal, Facebook & Co. have become a common, intergenerational environment. Yet it's true that if you know your current and prospective target clients, you will better manage your activities.

- The **best platform** to develop your strategy. There is nothing more wrong than thinking you have to be everywhere. Every social media has its own characteristics and rules, but above all it could be more suitable for a certain target or aim. For the same reason, a simple reproduction of the same contents on different channels never gives good results.

- Your **budget**. As the **latest update of Facebook algorithm** shows, social media are not free, which means that, like any other physical or digital channel, they require *ad hoc* resources.

WHY TO COMMIT SOCIAL MEDIA MARKETING TO A PROFESSIONAL

According to **"The State of Social 2018"** by Buffer, 74% of those interviewed who consider their social **media marketing activities useful** and **effective**, are mainly people who have invested in **paid** and **sponsored activities**.

If every SMM activity has to be deceived and incorporated within a precise strategy, it's better to commit it to a **professional**. As a matter of fact, among the **new digital professions**, one of the most requested by companies is the **social media manager**.

The majority of those who have invested in social media marketing and have a well-structured social media policy, can count on one or more social media managers who can be internal to the firm or even external consultants.

The **presence** of the social media manager in a firm is **transversal**: s/he collaborates with several departments and professionals (for example, the community manager), especially when it comes to front office and communication activities.

FROM CONTENTS TO ANALYTICS: WHAT IT MEANS TO DO SOCIAL MEDIA MARKETING

The daily routine of a social media manager is much more complex than you can imagine.

His or her main tasks (the activities needed to put social media marketing into practice) are **defining a content strategy** and developing an **editorial plan**.

Contents are the basis for building your digital presence and if you want to gain **involvement** and **visibility**, you have to ask yourself what is worthier for your fanbase: in this sense it could be useful to create personas (**protypes** of your **digital users**), similar to the **buyer personas** of the pure marketing. If you **constantly publish** new contents and find **the**

best times for your posts, you will be able to build client loyalty.

Even all the activities which contribute to create a lasting and profitable relationship with your **online community**, are an important part of a social strategy.

On social media, "as a client I expect to converse with the firm, to talk about my expectations and also to listen to its **vision**, its project, in a perspective in which the product becomes something collateral" SMM expert Claudio Gagliardini says during an interview.

This is why the social media manager should always work closely with the **community manager** and their activities should be part of a larger and integrated vision. Then, social media marketing has often to do with **influencer marketing**. The basic idea is to trust people (and their cluster of friends) or aspirational figures such as leaders, experts or professionals in single sectors, and to involve them in your social strategy to make it more profitable.

You can do it in many ways, for example through periodic takeovers of your social accounts.

SMM lives not only on social media activities, but also on **listening activities** and analytical activities. The firms who take the first steps on social platforms, tend to adopt a "passive" approach in order to understand what users are already saying about their product or what is the **conversational sentiment** about their brand. The **monitoring of the contents on social media** is also important for the next step and can be useful in several situations (when you develop or test a new product, when you have to face a reputation crisis or if you want to do **collaborative marketing**). Luckily, nowadays there are a lot of **tools for social media monitoring**.

Analytical activities are more structured and based on a series of *ad hoc* metrics. What factors do you have to take into account for **social media analytics**? It depends on your objectives. Anyway, it is safe to say that, besides rough and merely quantitative vanity metrics, more useful metrics exist which measure, for example, the **actual engagement** or the **return on investment**.

PROS AND CONS OF A SOCIAL MEDIA MARKETING STRATEGY

What are, in the end, the **advantages** of social media marketing compared to more traditional forms of marketing and advertising? It's important to understand that even the best SMM strategy can't survive by its own, as it needs to be part of a wider and more structured **business communication plan**. The **data on the advertising market** show that most investors have moved their budget from the analog to the digital, but **television**, **radio** and **printing** have not been abandoned yet.

The main advantage of social media marketing is its **little invasiveness**: more similar to the idea of **inbound marketing** than to the idea of interruption marketing, social media marketing reaches its addressees just where they are and, if done in the right way, it reaches them in those strategic **micro-moments** within the decisional process and the consumer "journey".

Other advantages of SMM are **more targeting**, more possibilities to reach micro-segments of audience and also to improve the less convincing aspects of the campaign along the way, starting from partial **performance insights**. This is why social media marketing is considered "a personalised and scalable marketing".

For these reasons, in 2015 there were already "2 million PMI that every month invested in the platform to make their brand grow.

Especially in Italy, where there are mainly small and medium-sized enterprises. To compete on the market, firms of all sizes belonging to all technical fields need innovative and easily accessible instruments which can offer an immediate return on investment". This remark refers to Facebook, ma goes for SMM in general, too.

If you consider the habits that are more and more characteristic of the Internet users (for example, **mobile-first content consumption**), you will notice that over the years all social platforms have wisely developed *ad hoc* and native instruments for mobile devices. Are there any pros and cons for this? It has been underlined that some SMM techniques – even if they can't be classified as **black hat** – are connected with **some ethical issues**: if you do **real time marketing** at all costs and in front of any kind of news, or if you use a provocative tone of voice, you could risk spoiling a good digital strategy.

There are a lot of famous social media marketing campaigns. Maybe, **Obama's campaign** for the American presidential election in 2008 is the most well-known: the republican candidate made massive and strategic use of social media which seemed, at that time, to be destined to change forever the face of **political communication** and, more in general, the rules of digital marketing.

Also the campaign #MakeItCount by **Nike** is considered one of the most efficient campaigns ever, together with **Ceres** for its **constant** and always attentive to the context **social presence**.

Not only big international brands, but also **smaller realities** and brands with territorial vocation have learned over the years to use effective social media marketing in their favour.

Anyway, there are some fields in which SMM reveals itself as one of the best channels to promote the product to the right audience: fields like **food&wine**, where content sharing on social media is strongly influenced by senses, and also the **cinematographic** field, where a **multimedia** and **participated** **storytelling** is necessary because of the **immateriality** of the product (i.e. the film).

CHAPTER ONE
Social Media Marketing Guide for Beginners

The method of social media marketing by which social media sites attract Web traffic.

During the process, typically creative content needs to be created to reach masses with ads from a trusted third-party source to share your interest material with others to establish a vicious chain that would cover businesses and go beyond the intended market audience.

Every online marketer must have an objective, a product, a service and a reason to promote the vast and overwhelming World Wide Web. If you've already defined these things in your mind, please!

This can probably be the hardest part of the social media challenge and from now on, every effort will help achieve these objectives efficiently and perfectly until you get to the position of a social media guru.

The world of social media is wider and wider than ever.

This is a highly strategic marketing platform reaching different cultures, ages, religions, sexes, locations, interests and so on, which makes it the perfect vehicle for reaching and targeting the right public and achieving total success. Video games are not important to the world, for example, but only people who play video games are part of their interests. If you target males with high-heel ads, maybe some of them would go to their wives and buy a pair or two, but a pair or two isn't exactly the kind of impact you want. We are therefore focusing on certain group ages and certain other variables that are making certain services and products, videos and news "viral." First, we need to be acquainted with the main social media sites of Facebook which have more than 900 million users. You can build and interact directly and openly with your clients, by using the services you want to provide or the product you are trying to sell, to upload free photos, products and videos. You can thus create a database of people who share your posts with their friends and thus create an endless chain. Most of these social media sites are electronic, so that users-whether it's a portable computer, laptop, tablet or phone-are always connected to the internet in a way that you can use. In any case, people log onto Facebook when driving, in the park, at home, at the school or work. Then you are there to advertise your company to be shown in news feeds and you would always be there to play tricks so that people will find something appealing and worthy of attention according to their desires. Some big companies such as Microsoft, Starbucks, Samsung, Rockstar, Pepsi, etc. do the same thing and it works perfectly!

Blogs Blogs are an easy way to communicate with people in semi-professional terms when it comes to content quality. The material of value is always the key to good writing and therefore good blogging. In less than five minutes you can get up and run your CMS (Content Management Service) blogger, some are Blogger, WordPress and maybe the most user-friendly, Tumblr. One of the tricks here is to know your audience, your business, who you are and what you want to achieve. All this has to do with the experience of SEO and Search Engine Optimization, that is to say, using the right keywords in a search engine as high as possible. Google, Yahoo. Google, Bing. It must apply to your posts and also ensure that you use a keyword search tool to test the competition and the number of searches in this specific keyword. The lower the competition and the higher the number of requests, the more convenient for you in a month. If you were to release your website with a technical support chat service, you would have to mention keywords to find you first for people seeking your service. It's technical support for Windows, for example, and then you have to use specific words to go a little straighter. Since the competition was strong and the support from Windows was a large material, you would focus and build on the special services provided by your company, adding additional keywords would be a successful way to do that, and you would be ranked higher in the search engine so people could easily find your product. From "Technical Support Chat" to "Technical Support Chat for Windows 7 and XP," you will learn how we are narrowing down the scope of service you provide, making it more general, more comprehensive and ultimately competitive in the mobile operating systems support market, cellular phones, Mac, iPhone, Windows Vista, Windows 8, etc. Once the keyword theory is known, you can continue and create content on a blog easily found by using the right tags on a search engine.

Then we're back in the blog room with Social Media integration. There are many ways to share your blog material. Some Content Manager Services like Tumblr can share or hate social media buttons. You must check for the options to activate (in the rare case, they are not available default), so every post of yours has the buttons you want to share within the blogging network to which you are associated with, Tweeter, Google+, Twitter, etc. With great quality and highly visual content, you inspire people to share their stories on other media sites, such as the ones mentioned above, and to post them.

Twitter An increasingly popular social media platform that is growing rapidly.

This website, with more than 340,000,000 tweets a day and about 140,000 users around the world, is very enticing for both companies, companies, and celebrities, singers, actors, all of them!

A tweet is an up to 140 character email that can be written and published and followers can read and display in their news feeds at any time.

Talking about it, engaging directly and starting new discussions is one of the things which makes this platform extremely effective.

Just as they do to advertising and marketing campaigns on brands and products of their interest, we will do to Kim Kardashian and read and think about everything she tweets in one day.

140.000.000 users can sound like a difficult task to reach the right audience, but when seen from the other side, it means more potential customers for a company. When you join any social media site's already described vicious chain, things only happen by themselves and you're first of all noticed by hundreds of people interested in your product, speaking about it, looking at it and asking others about activities, broadcasting and the like.

Linkedin Maybe a forum that is not so popular and boring for some, but the rest competent and strategic.

Those people will not spend long hours speaking and thinking about dumb and trivial things to others, rather, this social network goes straight to the point.

For example, people on Facebook or Twitter follow any of their interests purely for the sake of socializing as well as businesses, but Linkedin is supposed to filter and leave the fun to concentrate more intensely on social media expertise.

On Linkedin, you can be part of a work/service searching company or part of a work/service company.

You can create either a personal profile with your professional information, studies, contact details, interests, certificates, identifications etc., or, like yourself on Facebook or Twitter, make a business or a company page with the same purpose: share your brand, service, products information and keep your audience and followers up-to-date with the most updated ones

YouTube YouTube is a very interesting website. People watch any type of videos or are redirected via any website with a backlink to them or search engines.

Once you're there, you have a few "related videos" on a column on the right side of the screen.

Clicking from video to video makes you see things you never wanted to find, fascinating subjects, funny videos, how-to videos, ads, etc.

Your chances are incredible and people can also subscribe to your site, your own YouTube room for uploading your videos, in other words.

Often watching a video is much more fun and simpler than reading a whole text.

You have the visual tool.

You can, along with other choices, upload a video of people modeling your clothing, redirect people to your business website, advise people for shared content, subscribe for future video updates, visit your "fashion blog," like your Facebook page, follow you to Tweeter, Google+, Lin.

Close your eyes and try to imagine the entire Social Media Marketing Strategy Tree diagram and how it can touch that corner of the World Wide Web. Arbitrary, isn't it?

Google+ Google+ is a relative novice in the war against social media and offers a variety of products like Gmail, Google+ Basics, Google+ Circles that allow you to share information or' statutes' as Facebook does. You have a "Flow" feature like the news feed from Facebook which allows you to see what others are up to, which can be very similar to Tweeter.

The company is very desirable to professionals and business networks because products are exclusive and incorporated.

For example, you build a Gmail account and, if you disable it, you have automatic access to all these services and a profile that you can edit with a photo, contact information, etc.

You have access to the entire Google+ network including Gmail, YouTube, You+, Circles, Basics or even the popular search engine that saves and shows results for the most relevant things.

It is useful for any social media marketer to have a spare Google+ account because it has potential usability and because the origin of commercialization is not too small or too much.

Maybe you don't have the same effect, a TV ad 30 seconds as a tiny billboard on a bus, but the more you interpret the message the better results will be obtained.

According to the latest 87 social media marketing studies carried out by 2012, the approach from businesses to consumers known as B2C or Business to the Community was 16 percent higher and has the potential to grow to 57 percent in the next 5 years.

More than 30% of the world's population is now fully online and has eventual web access.

More than 1/5 of the free time is spent on social media sites, hitting some 250 million tweets and Facebook statuses updated daily.

More than 80% of active online users spend their money on social media sites and forums only in the United States. 60% of consumers use 3 or more types of online analysis comparing items, prices, and information about planned purchases, which account for 40% of those made on social media sites such as Facebook or just forwarded from one page leading to direct interactions with retailers about offers posted.

About 56% of Americans have one to three profiles in a social media site, 55% of them aged 45-55 and 70% of those with a search engine optimization (SEO) profile have organic data. 46 percent of all searches are for product or service information. Half of all regional mobile searches were performed. 66% of new customers are using local business search and online research.

There are about 863 million websites worldwide referencing' SEO.' The top two terms are' SEO products' and' SEO Business' and there are 9.1 million searches each month, including the acronym; more than 60,000 tweeters use' SEO' in their organics, there are 13 million blog posts which include' SEO' in their titles and Amazon.com holds around 2,700 books on SEO. 93% of online experiences start with a search engine.

B2B businesses that keep active content such as blogging and SEO services have on average increased their total website traffic by 25% in the last year, while those that have ignored SEO have seen a 15% drop overall in visits.

Web searches consume 21 percent of all time spent online. Google, Bing, and Yahoo! are among the top five search engines on the Internet. Given that AOL is #7 and Ask is #10, search engines are five of the top ten web sites most frequently visited.

Finally, social media marketing is an environment in which experts and advertising fans can come together and put their ideas and plans into action.

There is no university or college social media marketer, this information which should be gained through extensive research and evaluated continuously in the area desired.

It is a new approach that has moved the old tactics of television advertising to the online market.

The percentage of people who choose to go online on a laptop or a tablet versus people who watch TV continues to grow every day.

Statistics show that social media marketing has a lower impact than traditional advertising strategies, but its ability and scope for growth are without a doubt immense and could be far more engaging and enhanced than TV in the last decades.

The field of orthodontics social media advertising

The presence of social media every year seems straightforward to question most orthodontic

procedures aligned with the weapons-free rebellion and a clear objective. Many agreed because they did not know how even the first shot could be fired, to postpone entry into the rebellion. In all cases, you're not alone, and this is good news if any of these things happen. While most orthodontics have some form of social networking, very few people have seen their engagement pay off. And most of them do not understand the fundamental purpose of participation in social media; increase patient referrals by offering the "network" rationale, and incentives for integrating practical knowledge into their "network." Before entering the public discussion, their social media marketing plan recognizes the brand yet establishes the objectives of your practice. The answers could be different from "expertise," "efficiency," "modification," and "best words." Summarize the answers you can use to build personality characters, write down these attributes and share them with your team. This speaks not only to patients and families; it also tells the world that they are genuinely interested in their patients ' progress. If your profession is "investing in the community," enter the classroom in local training programs or talk to local teams on big games and take care of student-athletes whether they are your patients or not. Link to your local paper's honorary column. Write funny stories on paper. Login to the Digg RSS technology feed when the process "slashes down," and post new applications and social network tips on your comments. The training product is always connected to orthodontics in order to tell the reader something of a "voice" of practice. In fact, if his good opinion of the activities is improved and expresses it throughout his network, the reader reciprocates the value. How can I not say: you will be resolving your goods if your goal is to make people settle for your service. Clearly, any post that may be regarded as negative, imperceptible or unprofessional can tarnish the company's brand image and stop it. But there must be full ambivalence here too. Those in this training network know already that you are an orthodontist and plan to be published regularly on the issues of' braces-compatible foods' and' Southgate awareness month.'

In other words, it is a widely discussed subject: the optimal rate of posting. In many cases, too many are worse than too few. As a rule of thumb, it is more than once a day to post to a certain network, except in response to a comment or post string.

The average is once a week, but such a rare occurrence guarantees large posts.

Posting in the schedule is the optimal approach.

For example, Monday will be given to patients, activities and reported on Tuesday, press reports on Wednesdays and sports on Thursdays and/or weekend events. As specified, adhere to the schedule as strictly as possible. It is like product consistency.

Where do you say: the bulk of events took two Facebook and Twitter networks to choose from?

But in orthodontics, let's clarify them.

Facebook is the social network and Twitter is the microblog. As such, the search engine ranks of your website will be strengthened by Facebook for potential customers in the industry.

You can connect to your Facebook page for ease by simply posting on Facebook to keep both up to date. But there are other social media sites that need to be considered. Foursquare is a social network focused on locations where users can always check-in when they reach their smartphones.

When you sign in, announce the location of a message that will be sent on your Facebook wall. You will get hundreds of enrolments every day from patients on the walls of their hospital in dozens of posts.

Consider Flickr for and during your practice as the favorite place to upload all your pictures. Flickr's a network of users. Link your Flickr account to the Facebook page and the magnitude of your work has doubled.

How to encourage this: the most important way to increase interaction is to enable your participation in social media.

But, if you do it on Facebook, there is a strong warning phrase. Facebook has a wide range of guidelines that explicitly reject many types of orthodontic offers on its website.

Contests like "Upload and win on our wall" and "add a pixel to our Facebook pages" are infringements that would totally erase the user from Facebook if identified.

All the work done to develop the site would be fresh. To properly (and legally) conduct orthodontic contests or promotions through Facebook, third-party applications are required.

The full version of "Facebook advertising guidelines" can be found on the web. Few companies specializing in the manufacture of such products are, however, unique in that Orthodontic technology is primarily involved in the orthodontic sector.

How to simplify it: few applications allow all your social media accounts to be managed by a single Dashboard. The free version will suit most orthodontic procedures and save time and effort in managing the social media marketing strategy.

Where and how to Begin Social Media Marketing

This section will tell you where to start, what to do next, and how to build an excellent platform to update your social media networks to save you time. Don't look at this post as a high reading. You're going to delay. Begin with one social network, then move on to another, but really, stop and get on the car already. You have nothing to lose. You have nothing to lose.

1: Any Facebook organization ought to have a Facebook fan page. Period. Period. Facebook is the Internet's most visited website; yes, more traffic than Google. Potential customers spend a lot of hours on Facebook every day. The business page must be here so that they can locate it.

Next, build a Facebook fan page. Go through your biography pages and all the fields.

None of this information is private; everything is related to your business, so please complete everything. Do not forget to upload an image profile;

it might be your logo, an item, or another business element's picture. If you don't know what to use, use your logo.

You can get a vanity URL such as facebook.com/CaffeineKeyboard when your site has 25 fans. The first way to get fans is to put your mates on the page to help them enjoy it. Tap "Invite Friends" on the left top corner of your site to suggest this. Pages can only be indicated by site administrators.

The next move can both attract fans and shape the product. Turn to Facebook as your site instead of as an individual. Do this, use Facebook as a site, and pick your profile by clicking on Account. First, browse and "heart" other pages. Like pages you're involved in, other businesses you're interacting with, networking with, connecting with a family, clients, or mentors. The pages you want will be shown as pages on your fan page.

Now that there are more than 25 fans build your vanity URL on facebook.com/Username/ Allow your blog posts to be added to your Facebook fan page automatically (if you wish). Here is how: Go to the Facebook fan page app for Networked Blogs. In the top right corner, press "register a post" to follow the steps. That's it! That's it!

2: Twitter There are a lot of people I talk to who are new to Twitter in social media. The words used to characterize Twitter networking thwart them: post, hashtag, follow list, URL shortener, etc. The reality is you will get it in no time if you can give Twitter a couple of minutes a day.

A tweet is just a 140-character micro-blog post. When a reference is used, it is condensed so that it has fewer characters (URL shortener). Facebook is a straightforward way to keep tabs on a wide range of stuff.

Start with a twitter account on Twitter.com. Upload a picture, note that in a twitter stream, these are quite small and even smaller.

First, add your definition-this is a concise area, so choose your words wisely. Choose terms that describe clearly what you do. To reflect your brand, you should also modify your profile colors.

You are now going to "monitor" other Twitter users. The followers create the content that fills your tweet stream. You may search for specific people, businesses, or brands, or see what Twitter offers to follow.

Next, list, you put people in files and you build lists. You can have a person in a list, or you can't or obey them, so you can't have someone in an index. You may also choose to make the files open, which are available by anyone, or private (only accessible by you). Consider carefully the public records, how you name them, and who you have.

There are many WordPress plugins and website keys to tweet your latest blog posts automatically.

3: LinkedIn is a little less social media and a little more social networking. Each page of persons is identical to a Red Bull curriculum vitae (you can also export to print your profile). This is an excellent professional guide and platform for networking.

Start filling out your driven profile. The network should show what places you can fill out and try to fill in as more networking opportunities are developed. Attach all your job descriptions and past work experience–display your attributes; potential customers will study you!

Now is the time to add people to your network. LinkedIn may recommend a few users, but you should look directly for other ties. Think about past and current friends, bosses, mentors, school people, and even people you encountered in other social networks and welcome them to your system.

One of LinkedIn's great features is its classes. Tap on the top tab of the categories and look for your interests. There are classes for almost everybody's attention. When you join other communities, browse messages, comment, or "like," or even build your own. In these classes, there are a lot of things to say!

Continue LinkedIn activity through their add-ons in your profile. Many add-ons include blog posts and tweets, which appear in your profile and in the task feed LinkedIn, which keeps you powered.

Recommendations are the decisive edge. These are like testimonials of your work to be read by others. Go to "ask for suggestions" on the right side of your dashboard. You can choose who you want to ask; however, unwelcome suggestions can also be issued. Both guidelines can be reviewed, accepted or refused before others see them.

4: Google+ You've gone that far, you won't hurt one! Google+ has reached 20 million users faster than other social networks and is the newest social network. This network is different from the other three and user-friendly and forward-looking. Google+ only allows profiles of individuals, not businesses.

You put your friends here in "circles." You decide to name the circles you want (ex: friends, family, career, opportunities, news, etc.) and add people to the ring in question. If an individual is added to a circle, they will be notified that you have added them, but they are not told in which circle. When you browse your news feed, you can filter it around, just read family posts or news posts, etc. You can also choose who sees what you write, which circle of people can see what you type.

Cross market your profiles in social media-very important!

Support people to find you and all your social media profiles by directly linking them.

Here are only a few points where you can have profile links: email signature, including links to your social media profile with tiny icons and text links in your email signature.

Website: many websites have social media profile icons at the top of the page, on the left, on the contact page, or all three of them! When you choose to list your profiles in more than one region, use different media: one icon, another text connection, and another widget. It eliminates the appearance of doubling.

Blog: the same concepts as website profile listings except that at the bottom of each blog post, you can also add a link to your profile.

Profiles in social media: yes. Often people end up on your page, but it's not their favorite social network. The visitor can easily access your profile on their preferred network by listing your other profiles. Twitter is an exception, and the bio-section is too small to include and better suited for your data about your profile.

Social Media Advertising and Search Engine

Let us assume for a moment that you own a company and want to get people to find it online through search engines.

And we will also presume that you want to increase your company visibility through social media sites such as Twitter, Facebook, Pinterest, LinkedIn, Google+, etc. It is too easy to immerse yourself in the ocean of acronyms and misleading information related to the optimization of search engines, search engine marketing (SEM) and social media marketing (SMM).

Freelancers and self-proclaimed marketing "experts" often misuse the terms and exclude critical concepts. Add to it that Google is constantly changing its algorithms that decide the search engine rankings, and the applicability of information changes from one month to the next. The whole mess of jargon and conflicting information could be exasperating for non-technical business owners whose goal is to invest hard-earned cash on a well-considered campaign for online success.

Let's bring all of it is a relatively straightforward language any novice can understand. Don't overthink if a word or two eludes you. You're going to get the whole idea. After you have the basics down, you can "study" to learn more about each subject.

Here we go, Search Engine Optimization or "SEO" is a preparatory process to "optimize" the website to better index the content of the search engines. When we customize web content, we are following specific "thumb rules," and there are certain absolutes that we obey in compliance with Google's own "best practices" guidelines, which Google is so kind as to make publicly available to anyone who cares about doing so. Doing it correctly is affectionately called "black" hat SEO. To do it wrong or to manipulate and misuse the black hat SEO is labeled, just like white and black hats used in old western movies for "good guys" and "bad guys," respectively.

PREPARING the website with a correct SEO index is the first step towards effective site marketing. Around 2010, SEO and SEM are united under the term SEO. But, since then, the two disciplines have come together in their respective fields of tactics, techniques, and methods. SEO is "passive" but essential to the process of advertising. It is very critical that a page is well configured, but not "OVER-optimized," a phrase for sites designed to manipulate search engine results.

Google periodically changes the rules website administrators (webmasters and marketers) must follow.

Minor changes are often unidentified, but significant changes are usually labeled to draw attention to them and to explain categorically the types of modifications that are introduced so that Web practitioners can "think about" and see what types of marketing efforts are impacted on the same site.

For example, some of the Google names are "Caffeine," "Panda," and "Penguin" for algorithm changes.

The adorable sound of these names includes a set of rules and criteria which are affected by the change. For example, the latest move in Penguin 2.0 will have an impact on the overoptimized search engine rankings.

Optimization generally involves the adjustment of a website's text and link properties to include text position, keyword choices, website structure, page headings, keyword density, dilution of keywords, and many other considerations.

This is where the rules and the complete come into play. Also, Google provides very clear guidance on what is and is not suitable.

SEM is an advertising search engine. This is the active process of supporting a search engine website. If a page is being advertised without being configured in any way first, then the site is being promoted without being planned properly, like airing a TV commercial without editing it to clean up.

SEM comes in two simple tastes: herbal and subscribed.

Subscribed SEM includes elements such as pay-per-click, pay-per-impression, pay-per-placement, etc. When links are marked as spammy links, sites that are using paid links to promote the page will be struck by Penguin 2.0.

Think of paid SEMs as being equivalent to life insurance: if you pay your premiums (assuming good connection sources), however, if you discontinue your monthly payments, your search engine visibility from advertising sources is disappearing.

Organic SEM, on the other hand, creates additional independent web contents such as forums, posts, electronic press releases, photos, submissions to the directory, landing pages (not "doorway" pages), clear page mappings, and many other unique and original contents. Before using every organic marketing material for marketing purposes, it must also be optimized. You can see where this can become a process that takes time.

Organic SEM is not a "commercial" effort to put keywords and links on the Internet.

This requires creating value-added content that is appealing and useful to people who search keywords for topics on which you want to find your site, and so there is a double relevance: people's information and search engines ' value for keywords.

The quality of the advertising must be original, relevant, and unique. The amount of organic SEM for your company is to connect links from one source to another, enhance the traffic to your website and increase search engine rankings because of the high quality of the relationship and the resulting web content traffic. Also, the rules of thumb and certain absolute "do and don't" have to do with organic SEM.

Think organic SEM more like a lifetime insurance policy— Marketing costs are involved, but the accumulation of the original, independent web content doesn't go away over time, and the effect is often a Lasting, or rather a strong, lasting power for your site and its material— much as how the cash value eventually creates enough interest to support your lifetime policies.

The downside of the licensed SEM is that it's fast but typically more expensive. The downside is that the money you spend is short-lived. It goes away as quickly as it started.

The benefit of organic SEM is that it provides residual long-term effects that contribute to a good return on investment while saving money (if done correctly).

The downside is that it can take longer for saturation, a form of industry, geo-targeting, and many other factors to be identified.

BIG caution: the fields SEO / SEM and SMM are motivated by fraud and frustration. Because advertising is simply an advertisement, no ethical guarantee is available that a service provider can legally deliver unique site placements or tests.

That makes sense if you think about it. In Google page 1, there are only ten organic spaces for a selection of keywords.

If more than ten companies around the world (as well as other content concerning your industry) do what you do, and if at least 11 of them also pays for ads, how does the "guarantee" page 1, for a specific search term, results from an SEO / SEM provider?

In short, they can't— at least not ethically. But many THOUSANDS of freelancers and SEO firms are not discouraged by "empty promises in the dark."

Even marketing subscribed is not guaranteed. Another person can come and be willing to pay more for the place you want.

In a nutshell, it's "buyer beware" for SEO and SEM. Everybody wants your money. You want your cash. None trusts based on their say-so.

You need to be comfortable and confident about your relationship with the company you choose and the record you have set up with other customers.

The evidence is, so to say, in the pudding. Don't make a mistake other business owner make and make an emotional "buy" decision based on a convincing sales pitch. The talk is cheap. The talk is dirty. Make sure that anyone you consider can show meaningful results from a portfolio of other customers. Most people read a book and can "write." Remember: this is YOUR trade and YOUR dollars for marketing... So the provider you select must prove to be your trustworthy.

Regarding social media marketing, the old phrase, "word of the mouth is the best form of publicity," has always been a universal truth.

Consumers are much more inclined to buy on the advice of their friends and family than a paid ad to convince or change their opinions.

Our physical world has an online world in parallel: banking, dating, shopping, etc. View Social Media Marketing (SMM) as digital word-of-mouth.

To create RELATIONSHIPS with clients, you can grow an audience of fans, friends, and followers through Facebook, Twitter, Pinterest, etc.

It means creating a quest for people who are interested in "the things" that you post as they relate to their culture and interests.

Most social media businesses (or at least that's what they're calling themselves because they are a big moneymaker) are facing the problem of using social media as a point of sale. If each post, pin, and tweet is a kind of spammy, self-promotional demand that provokes people in your company, then your efforts in the social media will fail miserably.

Similarly, when you calculate the effectiveness of social media solely by the amount of "likes" and "follows," you miss the mark. The marketing company can easily pull the wool over your eyes and cite the sum of likes and follows as the secret to your success. The number of people who "like" you has zero-dollar revenue connection. Yes, it offers an indication, but between a "like" and the dollar, there is not a direct conversion... period. Period. And the number of people who like it is not as important as the total number of hits on your website. It is the QUALITY of hits, not the QUANTITY.

Sadly, "Sex, Drugs, and Rock & Roll" sells these days in society today. As for the advertising and general movement of search engines, when a site owner publishes advertisements and material promoting' free sex,' for instance, the linked website will certainly receive a lot of hits. But there will be no customers if the company does not supply or sell what the search engine is searching for. Some unscrupulous marketers may artificially make large amounts of traffic on the site via such unethical methods (though not exaggerated as the example I use here).

We use other (different) indicators to analyze SMM outcomes for ROI, but the study must be analyzed in a relevant context to determine how to participate in and use ongoing SMM marketing efforts. If not, it's only "busy work.

" In this way, most business owners simply do business-related blogs and so on, believing they are doing something positive with their marketing efforts (and trying to save money by not paying for a professional, experienced marketer), but unless the content is tailored and strategically adapted to their indeterminate web presence, it is mostly just wasted time.

There are lots of freelancers that like to talk to Facebook and Twitter and they think they can get away from charging companies with lots of money to make small conversations online through social media.

The findings were the same at the end of the day: the business owner invests more cash without ROI. Just because someone is confident and well versed in posting and tweeting through social media, it doesn't make them eligible to market your social media. You may have the best intentions, and you may feel you accomplish something by generating tons of "loves" and "followers," but unless you dovetail your other ads, you spin your wheels. Remember these points: acknowledging a "good landing" as a passenger on an aircraft does not qualify you as a pilot.

As a taxpayer, it does not make you a budget expert to know that government deficit spending is a bad policy.

As a Facebook user, making a profile that "likes" a bit doesn't make you a social media marketing expert.

The last thing is valid for many (if not most) applications from people who call themselves consultants and offer to make their campaigns in social media. You may feel that you're an expert who gets "likes" and fans for their comments, so you may think that you can make some money for other people and hang a shingle at your door to advertise yourself as social media marketers. Yet looking at one or two data points outside their scope doesn't qualify them more to do the job than admiring a smooth landing qualifies them to fly an airplane–or even just land it. There is so much more involved, just as effective online is involved.

Many unqualified freelancers and consultants pay much less when it comes to promoting their companies, so the temptation of spending your money with them is far greater.

Everyone loves a contract, okay? But if the money you spend does not achieve the expected outcomes, how much is it?

Further capital to produce a good, optimistic, and compounding return on investment would be much better spent.

The old phrase, "You have to spend money to make money" is there for a reason. Spend your money with wisdom.

Ask any contractor you are considering hiring a lot of questions. If they seem to fail, when they can't put things into context with your overall advertising or just "speak about," don't even DIE turn over your company to them. They're going to fail. You're going to fail.

CHAPTER TWO
How to Make Customers Like You

So you ask, what should I say or do, what should I like? You must first of all, be yourself. I made the mistake of trying to imitate a sound that seems "consuming" to my audience. When you're usually a little cynical (for instance), it may seem like a smart choice. But what happens is that it is difficult to assimilate the manner of someone else even though you might think you need it. Just be yourself, being successful is much simpler.

Also, the internet interactions of consumers must be excellent. Your page should be intuitive, and all the links work, a copy should represent keywords they are searching for and visually appealing. There are horrific websites out there (see Craig's list), but they are the exception. Confidence means that you have completed your website quest to solve their needs for more information. Do not trick them at first, or you may never see them again.

1. Blogs / Websites In recent times, businesses have a clear tendency to put their blogs ahead of mainstream websites. Why? Why?

Because these companies know that, if customers like you (or your company), you will be more optimistic and eventually selling. In other words, the voice means confidence, and trust means sales. Because your web store is your blog and website, you need to stand up for your customers to address their needs.

In the early stages of the sales cycle, you work to ensure that they are knowledgeable of you and have the right information for them. The primary education is that you are a credible source. If you explain how to address your problems, they will be much more open to sharing their issues. So, you will use your blog to demonstrate your passion for solving and moving their questions as best you can with a comment (your response).

This needs to be included in your blog copy and photo.

2. There is nothing like face-to-face, old-fashioned discussions on topics of interest, so people know what you're made of. While it might seem like working for several people, meeting people physically is a great way to spread your impact on the Internet. Meeting teams are communities of particular interest on all continents.

Whether it's rock climbing, lizard collection, or waistcoat, there are groups in your area on the web site of Meetup Groups that provide an excellent way to give your personal touch.

Each community has a website, and many of these groups allow open messages to the whole group. As usual when sending messages to unsolicited individuals, it's better always to ensure that your letter contains material that is of general interest to the audience and not that your service is marketed.

And note, we try to make you happy. You need to like it before you buy it. They can use their network of people to spread the word if they like you.

3. Whether you are using Linked In, Twitter, MySpace, or any other Web 2.0 assets, you are as intimate as you are on the web as possible in terms of the ability to use photos. Let people see you and hear you talk about their desires if you want to be content. Make sure you always mention what kind of answer they are looking for and how your solution answers it — Youtube the easiest way to do this. Many people's videos are shy.

It takes many times when you first film videos to feel comfortable in front of your camera, but then you become average. It's best to make a video with your digital camera or mobile phones.

Upload the clip to YouTube, ensure that it has a niche keyword. Why? Why? Because YouTube the second highest search engine in the world (after Google, of course). This means that more people are looking for things on You Tube than on Yahoo. Use your You Tube code to embed the video into your website and elsewhere.

4. Flickr.com is the most famous photo-sharing site on the web. Flickr is a free service and uses if you have one, your Yahoo account name. Otherwise, you can make another. The benefit of Flickr is that 1) you can use these images in any web activity–e-mails, forums, chat groups, Twitter messages, and other, and 2) Flickr helps you to get to know you on another site.

You have a kind of different presence as a video with images. Images, however, allow you to cover a lot of ground quickly. You likely already have many digital pictures of your holiday, friends, family, food, cat, home, garage band. You can use any of them to improve the brand you are promoting. Remember what brand is - it is your intestinal reaction, your goods, desires, and your approach to a cause. Make sure it is accurate and use images to boost it.

5. Content Aggregation What is the aggregation of data? Content aggregation is of interest to your staff (for example, clients) when you knowingly

consume publicly available internet content (blogs, forums, videos, presentations).

Your customers profit from stopping them from gathering opinions and data. They also benefit from reading your feedback on this information in previous reports.

The benefit is that when you display this content, you keep it on your screen. You don't want them to leave your website (your store) to pursue stuff.

Content aggregation helps you to appear to support their issues while constantly modifying your service. It also provides objective opinions and information from other experts who confirm their intellectual knowledge of their needs and how your solution relates.

Marketing Inbound What do I mean by marketing inbound? This is your input in your sales practices in order to serve your clients better.

When you find that consumer traffic on your page is not expected (a high bounce frequency, for example), it's time to reflect on why. You talk directly to your customers.

I encourage you to use the term "you" in your copy when you speak with your audience instead of just referencing "our customers.

" If not, ask your friends, family, and close colleagues to review your blog to see if you have any issues. I know it's tough. It might be that your blog's length, colors, copy, or tone does not meet the standards.

Measuring how well customers like you While it's a struggle to know how well you like in your niche web transactions, there are some telling signs.

If you get traffic to your blog, do you have people who sign up or comment on your posts?

If not, it might not mean that you or your cause do not like them.

It may mean that your writing does not include them or that you spend so much time selling your brand at the cost of interacting as people with them. Listen to a link in the tone of the comments.

Will you sound like you realize that you have taken their interests? You may have questions regarding rival alternatives or product features or how to purchase, but these are not "like questions."

5 Ways to Be the Best Option for Your Customers

Here are the best choices for using Web 2.0 assets to make your customers prefer your brand with social media marketing: 1. Blog / Website, first, I suppose you have a website or blog to sell your product directly through internet marketing. If you don't have one, you must make one. A blog or website is straightforward to create these days. If you're a dead beginner, Word Press Direct is the one I recommend that you use. Word Press Direct allows you to create a blog that will enable you to create advertisements and ads for other widgets. It is so easy that you can use your website for free in a day (or less) using your software. You make three free websites, and you even host them.

You will have a sales section on your website or blog. Others call it a money page. You can channel customer traffic to your website. It will also be the site from which you tap to finish your order.

The money page is usually the site with the "Buy Now" key, or a link can be clicked on.

Your site has a friendly and knowledgeable copy that discusses the decision-making considerations that draw your attention. You must analyze and understand the problems or concerns your customers have. The ad copy also offers general answers to the solution and the specific features of your company. You must, therefore, give your clients an obvious path from the challenges to the benefits that make sense for your company.

Here are some specific elements that can be used: Comparison Tables-use a table that displays consumers ' strengths and contrasts you with the next innovative solution. Make sure the incentives are solutions to your critical problems.

You don't need to name your competitor, and I advise you that you don't do this unless your competitor is very strong (which already is kicking the ass on your market). Instead of using text, use checkmarks in columns.

2. Competition Sites If you don't find the keyword phrase on the first search page in Google, you need to look closely at the rivals on the first page. Sign up to receive free entries (newsletter, white papers, downloads) on the pages of your competitors.

Read your emails and learn what your customers are thinking. You must determine what your rivals say to their clients and tell them. See if your competitors have a blog in which you can post content or comments on performance.

There is nothing wrong with posting answers or comments on their pages intentionally. Pay particular attention to and comment on critical pain points through visitors ' posts. You can have a link back to your website/blog on your signature line. This is also an excellent way to build a connection with your competitors and clients. Be cool; it's fun to do more.

You might also have heard about a trackback's internet technique.

This is web software that links your competitors ' blog when you post on your own! Find out whether trackbacks are allowed and if so, you want to use them. Post a link to your website and benefit from the traffic created from your post.

3. Discussions/forums Make sure you're talking at social media sites where your competitors already speak. If you search Google (or YouTube) add either the words ("discussion," "topic," "video" or "blogs") such as "torture raising discussion," or "turtle raising forum" to your niche so that you can list your competitors and customers already. You should engage in this dialogue and become recognized. Feel free to post comments of high quality. Groups on Facebook, Linked, My Space is also available.

Again, at this point in the buying process, you must ensure that you post on issues relating to critical problems your customers face.

In the case of turtle selection, it may be that some turtle species have been inaccessible and that others in the industry have been treated inhumanely. Speak about these things and be a voice of thought. Remember to use a signature and link to your website. Sometimes the top competitors refuse the positions. Report on the second level of competitors. In that case.

4. Inbound Marketing Use your customers ' data in improving your details and content. Inbound marketing means listening (and enhancing your message) to your customers (and competitors). Internet marketing is different because it allows you to be in business from scratch every day.

I've done this several times before.

In doing so, you can be sure that you will have plenty to know from the box after one day. Now what used to be "ready, goal, fire" is "ready, fire, goal." A good marketer is continually adjusting. Competitiveness requires versatility.

5. Preference Measurement The fact is that others compete in the same market niche as you. The goal now is to ensure that your customers prefer your approach to others.

Once, it seems to be a straightforward statement. Nonetheless, in open discussions and talks, the job is to determine the mood or behavior of the community.

Do your questions seem to meet your needs, or does it take a lot of persuasions? If you must sell your customers in real-time person by person, this tends to be a considerable job which takes your precious personal time every day. Ad copying should be quick and resolve the problems beforehand.

Major Updates in Social Media Marketing

You see it on YouTube — Google's announcement at the I / O conference this May of Google TV and Google Internet services was not just announcing another launch, or yet another previous acquisition, that had turned into vertical Google.

She was adamant about how she intends to rule every part of the world's lives through the W3, of course. His promise to boost the Web faster without crashing throughout the globe and to add a TV service suddenly changed the whole perception of the world wide web and how it was a place of time for teenagers.

For YouTube as popular as its search engine for parents, it had a great platform to provide YouTube with a growth hormone by initially splitting it into sub-channels, just as other social networks had a single profile page.

After everyone wanted to promote their channel on the video site, they had accomplished, "When you haven't seen it, you can watch it on YouTube.

" Over the past few years, it has been the most frequently visited place to view any incident reported still or video in the world.

You wanted to learn something that presentations are available on YouTube, teach something you can post there, chat about something like a funny accident or an unusual occurrence, or an awe-inspiring historical moment, such as the World Cup or the summer Olympics or the opening presidential YouTube is your spot.

Live streaming is sports, big natural disasters like earthquakes and hurricanes, and when news breaks down, why not go to our television channel first? Because YouTube has earned the reputation of being the place where you can see the real thing in an uncensored version.

If you're an entertainer, it's just as popular as your latest video downloads. Today Google is about to turn YouTube to a lean-back TV on your computer or an online channel that you would rather have to search your TV in real-time.

Can you imagine that TV will lose its appeal when print media has sunk into online media? You want to make it big in social media marketing. All that you need to do is use the shovel is your gold mine.

Twitter + Facebook joins SEO for real-time searches—the entire web environment is evolving, and search engines also need their energy, as with any news media.

With millions of talks happening all over the world over almost anything under the sun, the real data comes from people who talk and not from news reporters.

This year, companies like Google, Bing, and Yahoo have been looking for twitter feeds and for the Facebook news feed.

If you are looking for something, not only are sites available on this topic but also what was tweeted or posted on the wall of someone. If your company has your twitter product / Facebook profile, the updates will enter the same SEO pipe, so that they check in real-time. Last year your tweets were only 140 characters of catchy short messages, today they are 140 keyword characters rich in the hungry search engine information.

Think of your current social network marketing slogan before you tweet or update your product page wall.

Only one convergence has boosted organic traffic for online companies and online sales firms.

This also influences other social networks, such as geolocation searches and map uploads, open the Facebook "like" graphics on forums, blogs, and photo galleries like a flicker.

Everything will eventually be brought to the quest ocean.

Is there a requirement for it? You can always install other software if you have a smartphone to make life easier.

Ios, blackberry, Blackberry, Symbian belt as many applications on your mobile for as many jobs and various activities.

Smartphones are now the core for trade, media, communication, data use, payment, and networking. With so many life activities on a palm-size phone, should there be an app to get well, sleep without snoring, right??

There's one on iTunes, I'm sure. You are really smarter by hour today; not only do you use Twitter, Facebook and 4square on your mobile, but also pay charges, sync your calendar with your friends or associates, video calls, photo sharing, brainstorming, preparing for activities, exchanging plans, accessing bank accounts, authenticated QR code security checks with other telephone calls. Today, mobile is everything you need to communicate and network in events. Do you recall that you would ensure an expensive leather case with robust and trustworthy business cards at any event in your pocket? Okay, you don't have to load yourself or the world. Get bumped into the other device.

Online business cards catch up very fast, because the physical ones take an effort, of course.

Outlook incorporates Facebook—Okay, who recalled the awful day your boss took you on Facebook social networking? You can now laugh loudly because the promotion of social media makes it imperative for people to connect to social media sites such as

Facebook in real-time to achieve more conversion and more company input.

Let us face it when we are excited and involved; productivity is high.

Outlook has prevented you from leaving your workplace and signing up on Twitter.

Today, if your Facebook and Outlook ID are the same, you can incorporate it into your view and chat with your fellow Members in real-time, without emails or phones. The interaction has the persona of the people on your network since it's all online. The whole idea looks fun for consumers, but, of course, Google this year had given a Wave. Google Wave is a new way to operate and operate a cloud office. You may formulate proposals, refine them, organize them, analyze the advantages and disadvantages, make an action plan, and carry through the program for success or otherwise. You can all be in your respective areas (the same office building) or separate continents, and wave makes it possible for a long-distance team to work without any barriers.

Wave is a whole new range of Google cloud technologies that Microsoft recently revealed and launched. Now Wave is available, but I haven't heard about people shouting and making this great app for you.

CRM replacement customer development programs—Customer relations management are making a difference. Your brand is distributed over at least two or more social networking websites, not to mention other online marketing sites and search. Today the dashboards give you an overview of how people connect, speak about you, and associate you with your product. Public management helps your brand a better understanding of what your business and brand have been told and perceived. It helps you to monitor your audience by using a dashboard to communicate, interact, and discuss your needs on different accounts and social network profiles. Involver, Hootsuite, Tweet deck are several different platform styles and levels to explore

CHAPTER THREE
Successful Social Media Marketing

Here are seven secrets that go beyond all social networks and enable you to apply them in ways that your business grows regardless of the field in which you are:

1) You must take your company where the people are and talk to them. And the related discussions take place in social media in the world today.

With different companies, individual networks will be various. Someone in the business sector must be on LinkedIn, and a band is still a better candidate for a MySpace page. The criteria on which social media sites you must be is simple: where are your customers and prospects today?

When you understand what those sites are, ensure that you are there, and contribute to the community. Be sure that you can be identified as you check for your area of expertise.

2) Have an attitude, you likely have a confident manner when you're a company selling accounting software to accountants and other marketing materials. When you market exotic cars or couture style, the atmosphere would be very different. Whatever this environment, all social media accounts will bleed.

This attitude will appear in all your graphics, such as your Facebook fan page header and photo, your avatar image, and wrap on your Twitter page or even your heatstroke style on your LinkedIn profile.

I can't count how often people have been talking to me or sharing one of my posts, and when I click on their page to see if I'll follow back, I wonder... None. Nothing. No photo, no organic, not even the town in which they live. But if you hope to build your brand with the help of social media, extend your reach or make money, give us something to do.

You can start with a photo!

If we're heading to your twitter page and there's only a colored egg on the back of your head, it's like a billboard which says, "Hey, I'm Amish, and I'm wondering if it's going to end with this software fad!" Please ask somebody if you don't know how to upload a photo.

Consider it a real image of you, not of your dog or cat or fire. And add a new one, please.

(Don't be one of those who send a pic and show up fifteen years later!) We want to know with whom we're talking to, also with cartoons or icons. Use them only if they are an essential part of your branding.

And by the way, your avatar should be your username for many of you reading this. But don't do it at all. Think of who is making the feed and if a personal picture would be good instead. You could put the icon on the website somewhere else.

The atmosphere should also be reflected in the copy. Lang Lang's profile on Twitter could include conservatories of music and orchestras with which he has played.

Most significantly, the brand's atmosphere and mood should be the best in the feeds you post.

The feed will suit who you are.

You expect inspirational tweets to accompany Joel Osteen; you sometimes expect doses of snark when you read Bill Simmons. Ensure that your social media posts fit the message (and feel) that you deliver across all your platforms.

3) Engage, do not broadcast.

There's a justification for not broadcasting social media. So, stop broadcasting and talk to the people. Nobody wants to follow a feed that is nothing but pitches for any company.

However, if you make your feed valuable and relevant, people don't mind making an offer for your products or services occasionally. Nevertheless, considering the problems they solve for your customers, it is always easier to view them rather than the features of what you offer.

The most advantageous social media offers are the relationships with your tribe. Providing real value through your posts is a safe way to do this.

The "real value" is determined by who you are and what you are offering. If you are a building contractor, followers would also like to see ideas for construction and renovation. If you're Bill Maher, it's probably real quality known as witty quips.

Post durable material, informative remarks, and interesting talks. Commit your backers, exchange comments, and be part of the community.

Here are some examples

Suppose you are a seller of appliances, and you have a new model fridge for sale.

Some companies are merely beginning to broadcast sales pitches such as "New X KitchenPro refrigerator available" or launch their races with offers such as "Save $100 on the X KitchenPro refrigerator model."

What about a blog or YouTube video about lowering the energy bill and showing how the energy savings the new KitchenPro refrigerator offers are?

What about a local nutritionist or chef writing about the advantages of healthy eating by discussing the temperature-controlled crisp drawers, large storage area, and other benefits of the new refrigerator? You can then publish articles on the forum, provide some value, and sell your new product simultaneously.

Suppose you're a designer of a website.

You may undoubtedly send some posts announcing that you are developing websites.

What if then you wrote a blog or video, including some case studies of the clients you work with and how the websites you built have expanded their scope and profits?

You may highlight those features developed by you that helped optimize the search engine, user functionality or other benefits. You are the leading authority on your profession to provide detailed case studies and quality like this, and you will finally get more work.

Sure, an ice cream parlor, pizza shop, or yogurt store can trumpet new tastes through social media.

But how much more successful it would be if a social media campaign were produced in which users would suggest and vote on their feelings. ?

Can you remember the first blowing of the internet, and everyone thought about three "Cs" of information, culture, and trade? Today, it's not so unusual. When you write things that are important to people, they will follow you. And if you prove that you are part of the family through communication, sharing, and interest-the business will naturally happen to you.

If you have a large company, you will need a lot of different social media accounts run by different people. An aviation company could need one Twitter account for the customer service, one for elite fliers, another for dealers and specials, and one for flight updates. A college could have one from the president, a few others from professors, one from the administration, and others from different departments.

4) Nobody can keep up with all social media platforms. Where to place your flag Look for main words and terms to see where the discussions are headed. Look at your best customers and see where they invest their time on social media.

Choose one or two channels that you choose and focus on them. Let your family know where your time is spent. Ask them when you upload a YouTube video daily or once a week or once a month. If you're checking Facebook first in the morning and not the rest of the day, put your profile correctly. You're going to follow you there as you let people know when and where you are hanging out.

5) Test your product.

Use a third-party app to create a column that monitors any time you or your business is listed. You will know what delights consumers and be able to reward the responsible workers. You'll also know immediately if bad stuff happens, and you can step in to repair it. This instant feedback is invaluable and offers a summary of how the practice and product can be enhanced.

Through social media, people will talk about you whether you want them or not.

It's insane not to listen to them. It never stops shocking to me how many businesses spend millions of dollars on market research and focus groups, but are utterly oblivious to the social media, so that they can gain even more information for free.

If you do not respond to a brush fire in social media, it easily becomes a wildfire and anti-social press for you. When you see a problem early on and work to solve it, opponents can quickly become raving fans.

6) Be Real. It works in two different ways with social media: who makes the posts and the use of automated or aggregated content.

Make it clear who posts on your account. Whether we track Twitter or the Taco Bell Facebook page, we presume the marketing department writes the posts.

If we follow Richard Branson, we expect that jobs will be from him unless otherwise specified.

For some CEOs and other public figures, this is a delicate balance. For example, Sir Richard has over three million followers. No response to any direct message and query can be expected. (And, Richard genuinely succeeds in engaging in a remarkable amount of contact with his followers.) If you are a public figure with a large audience, you should model what other public figures such as President Obama and singer Keith Urban do. Your staff keeps their feeds, but their tweets have their initials. This type of arrangement works well because it allows staff to post ads, upcoming events, or promotions, but also enable the public to connect to their supporters.

What doesn't work is when a person develops a social media account, then tries to make it work for someone else. For example, a tech-shy CEO feels left out because his grandchildren don't talk about Twitter. He has set up a page and post tweets to his assistant. Since his posts are not actual, there are no links, and from that rarely comes anything good. (Probably insipid inspirational quotes.) Which leads us to post automatically...

There are applications to post multiple sites simultaneously and to schedule updates later.

This isn't a good thing necessarily.

Be aware that you are most likely restricting their reach when you use a service that sends your messages to multiple platforms.

Sites like Facebook allocate comments from aggregators to a lower level, which makes them much less likely to appear in feeds of followers.

And people who use these services are often unaware of the cultural and format differences among different platforms. Facebook is more personal, not LinkedIn. Not many posts work well across all platforms. And a lot of content on Facebook is cut off by the Twitter character limit.

As for self-scheduling messages, it is like sending a robot on a networking Chamber of Commerce to distribute the business cards. Hopefully, it is useful, but is it likely to deliver the results you want?

Last year a dear friend I followed on Twitter died. Sadly, three weeks after her death, I got some automatic tweets from her until her family finally shut up the account. Those tweets made me feel more the agony of my loss.

This does not necessarily mean that you should never schedule posts automatically.

It may be helpful to have certain advertisements or announcements at certain times. But a fully automated account is nothing more than a new channel for broadcasting, and followers will soon get settled.

The auto-scheduled tweet from an airline the asks people to vote for the flight attendants ' favorite new uniforms is 99% adorable. But if one hour after one of its plane's flies, the company looks inept at best, heartless, and at worst insensitive. Therefore, even when harmless updates are planned, remember to interrupt them.

7) Infect the Advocates Artists are cutting off the intermediary and connecting them through social media with their tribes. Another case study is Cody Simpson, the Austrian man who conquers the world and tweets the world one by one.

His record company noticed him after uploading his performances on YouTube. Today, he said, "Music can only benefit you. Many carriers have been produced online on Twitter, YouTube, Facebook, and Instagram, and they think it is essential to keep the content up and hydrate fans.

Effective Social Media Marketing Request for Proposal

Each segment offers a short description of the RFP and social media project company and the ideal working relationship.

Provide the necessary information to enable vendors to prepare a precise offer.

When you think there is some confidential or other information you would not want to publicize, you need to sign a Non-Disclosure Agreement before the data is received. This may restrict the involvement of vendors, but often private information needs to be protected.

1. Company Overview Your business goals Your company's history through social media or why your organization wants to start social media

2. Overview of the project State project goals and how they relate to the above-mentioned business goals. Explain the desired form of seller relationship i.e., Project-based, Record Company, etc. Explain the current involvement of your organization in social media and how it relates to the principal presence of both your organization and any associated campaigns.

Explain the social media channels you would like to use the drive if you are not searching for suggestions, then specify to the sellers how the project fits in with your overall marketing.

3. An overview of markets and stakeholders List the company's primary targets, i.e., demographics, psychographs, etc. List fundamental knowledge

needs of each target group Identify whether a consumer or public study is needed in carrying out the campaign 4. Overview: Make it clear what kind of answer you're looking for: are you looking for a theoretical solution or a clarification of how the seller would build your project. Many times, a suggestion is not the best way to approach an RFP simply because a company requires some critical pieces of information that could negatively affect its ability to recommend a certain solution. To order to provide a level playing field for all eligible vendors, it is crucial that a timetable is easily followed, both when the RFP is published, when and to whom questions are appropriate and when and in what format answers are needed Specify the most detailed responses and weight the effectiveness of past customers ' work.

If your PSP is published publicly, it will allow those requesting RFPs on Google or through other methods to locate the applicable request for proposals.

All interested vendors must optionally register their intention to send a proposal by a certain date, typically within 1-2 weeks of the PSP.

This is a great way to limit the possible number of sellers who respond to many proposals and choose to obtain a smaller quantity.

They recommend that the question and answer period ends at least one week before the proposal is scheduled.

It is up to you to answer questions via e-mail, conference call or mobile.

To ensure that things are as equal as possible, we encourage you to share all the questions (and answers) with all interested sellers.

Also define which type telephone call, email and who should be answered for these questions. We suggest that a single person be established as the point of contact in your organization. Simply ensure that holiday schedules, etc. do not interfere with this process, and if there is any other purpose the primary point of contact will need to be out of town during the process, create a secondary contact point for responses from issuer to be sent in the following formats by 20XX. Such meetings shall complete by XXth, 20XX Awarding the chosen vendor by XXth, 20XX Research to start by 20XX and to last until (as appropriate) questions and skills of a vendor The following questions are asked by the vendors making proposals if applicable. Some may not be applicable, but it is a good idea to get as much idea on social media as possible of the vendor's approach and philosophy.

Compare the feedback and the work and reading done to ensure that the seller is up to date with the latest opinions.

COMPANY DETAILS Other location(s) Primary phone number website and blog URL Primary point of contact (name, name, telephone and e-mail address) Total number of staff Sales representatives whose primary function is social media C

Please list your experience of social, paid and earned media integration. Does your company specialize in a sector or type of work?

SOCIAL MEDIA MARKETING STRATEGY Please describe your social media strategy process Which stakeholder groups are typically part of a strategy commitment? Please list and provide links to your company's primary media channels (e.g., blog, Twitter account, Facebook group, blogs by managers, etc.).

Describe the end outcomes of a campaign commitment.

What is your overall social media strategy for integrating existing applications, blogs, microsites, and newsletter programs?

How do you guarantee the consumer laws are complied with?

Describe your approach to the convergence of brand advertising, customer service, and corporate communications. How can you turn a typical product into a two-way dialog? Please give an example of your work in this field?

Please give an overview of your strategy work leading to an initiative on social media and business results.

What is your system for product and credibility monitoring (e.g., proprietary software used, methods, etc.)?

What do you think of robotic feeling analysis? Which kind of technology? are you using to help you monitor online?

How long (on average) is it between posting and being flagged to the customer?

What have your company dealt with in the past (e.g., 2,500 references per week)?

How does the quality assurance system guarantee the active and reflective handling of the vast volumes of data collected in the testing process?

Please explain your digital crisis handling approach. Which tools do you offer to support online crisis management?

Please describe your crisis management team structure, including biometrics and relevant experience. How do you determine what references require immediate responses and which do not?

Please provide a case study detailing your job for reputation or online crisis management, including results and learned lessons Please include a sample of your monitoring report format and a link to the appropriate dashboards (specifics should be removed) METRICS, MEASUREMENT & REPORTING

You have developed proprietary metrics? Please include specific examples based on past work? How did you apply these to customers?

How did you define return on investment (ROI) in the past from the perspective of social media?

How do you take data from various social media channels and measuring methods and merge them to give you an objective / exhaustive view?

What is your approach to database management and user analysis?

Are you able to measure costs per lead or costs per purchase? Please give an example of a project in which you did this. Which instruments can you not accurately measure from or only provide small measurements?

Please provide a sample calculation file or final report (specifics should be removed) What budget percentage is the measurement and measurement recommended?

CLIENT EDUCATION & TRAINING Do you provide clients with social media training? If so, in which formats are they available?

Which internal processes are in place to ensure that staff are kept up to date on technology and best practices in social media?

How do you measure progress and assess the effectiveness of training?

How do you suggest to consumers to keep up to date on new trends and best practices in social media?

SOCIAL MEDIA OTHER DIGITAL CHANNELS How do you model, build and handle the community?

How much of the team works towards developing and delivering social media strategies versus management and consulting?

Your experience with the platforms and tactics-YouTube and related video-sharing sites-blogs, audio-players, vodcasts, forums-Customer Relationship Management (CRM)-Search Engine Optimization (SEO) and Search Engine Marketing (SEM)-Facebook pages, applications, API integration-Mobile application creation-Twitter-N-Please describe your experience with the following platform and tactics:

How do you assess and identify "influence?" How does your contact process include defined online influencers?

Which tools and techniques do you use to handle the relationship of influence? How have you incorporated influencer outreach into mainstream communications and/or marketing campaigns?

How do you approach talks between stakeholder groups?

When you get a project done, what is your exit strategy for influencers?

How do you maintain integrity and honesty in the delivery of customer service?

Please provide a case study of the CLIENT SERVICES & PROJECT MANAGEMENT online community outreach project. How is a standard client interaction organized for your company?

How are the customer teams structured?

Please describe your system for internal communication.

If your account staff is separate from your project management personnel, please explain in detail how these teams work jointly If you are selected to provide social media services, who will be assigned to our company (provide names, titles and short biographic notes).

What is their role?

How priced are your projects? Do you use an hourly rate? Blended level of agency? If the latter, please provide a rate card What shifts the company employs in management practices?

What reports will be made available to the client to report project milestones and overall project health?

How often are these reports?

What is your business requirements collection process?

Writing a request for a proposal (RFP) is an excellent first step in evaluating the work of social media and online advertising since careful planning is needed to identify and build an effective integrated campaign.

A well-thought-out and performance RFP is important to a productive project because it lets you concentrate on your priorities and how they can be accomplished.

Social Media Optimization Rules

Social Media Optimization applies key elements to your websites or content to promote their dissemination across large social networks.

1. That your linkability Linkability is ready to connect to your website from other websites or posts.

One way of raising your natural Google listing is to increase the number of authority sites linked to you so that you can make your website more informative and accessible to others to increase your connection with social media optimism. You can do so in many ways: forums, white papers, press releases, keywords, RSS feeds, etc. This is the most important step in optimizing social media and should be your priority.

2. Easy to tag and bookmark the action of tagging is to bookmark social bookmarking websites for the website.

If you like the products or services on a website, for example, you tag them. Attach the tagging links to other pages of your site (not just a homepage) and make sure that when visitors press the tag button, there is a feedback box that will help your user list a tag and a message.

3. One form of improving your natural social media listing with Google is to get more backlinks.

This can be accomplished by improving the relation between people / websites (inbound links). Inbound links are links that send people to your page from elsewhere. One way to reward people for having a "recently linked" link to your site is by listing all websites that have a link with you.

4. Support your brand leverage social media to provide the audience with useful content.

You need to help you reach as many people as possible when publishing content like an article, a video, or an audio file.

You can do this through the request to the related websites for high traffic. You receive backlinks to your page when the word gets out about your great content (no matter what format).

5. Encourage the use of the content on two websites and mash them together.

YouTube makes it easy to mix your content (videos) to your page, for example. Moreover, because it is so simple, you have added a video to your website that contains a YouTube logo and a link back to your tube.

To encourage social media optimization, other sites can use your content conveniently and connect to it to redirect traffic to your page.

6. Even if it doesn't support you, be a client tool.

Honesty is something that all visitors appreciate. With the optimization of social media, you should link to other websites to help your visitors to achieve their goals or to find the information they want.

Do this, even if it's not for you. By linking to competitors or non-created content, you profit from the comprehensive data on a specific subject. Finally, more people will relate to you as you have lumped all information (or links) in one location on a topic.

7. Helpful and useful users Reward Your best friends are valuable users.

A helpful user can be detected in several ways, bringing traffic to your website, adding relevant content, or supporting users on your page.

No matter what they do, you can reward them if it benefits you, your site, or your service.

This can be done by sending a personal message to thank you for your dedication.

Another way of rewarding your valued users is by developing reward systems, encouraging them, and supporting their contributions on your website.

You can engage by joining the conversation on your topic (or selected keyword) with Social Media Optimization. It's not going to keep the buzz of posting articles and sharing information.

On other websites, you can continue to share information.

Your engagement helps share your knowledge with more people.

One way to do this is to find people commenting on your topic and to add to the discussion.

Participate in forums or other social groups that discuss your topic. Read and respond to comments on your posts, videos, and audios.

9. Know how social media marketing targets the audience by sharing content/information.

Not everyone is interested in your subject, so make sure your marketing research is done and that you post your information and knowledge where it is understood and appreciated.

10. Content is regarded as any information form that benefits a visitor. Content can be a white paper, document, image, audio, button, list continues.

Your job is to find a piece of content that will draw visitors ' attention.

Regardless of which market you join, there is always a type of content that you share with others. Figure out and give it to them. In turn, they will come back for more useful content. If this happens, you know that your optimization of social media is successful.

11. Real Internet users are searching for certain content on the web. When you supply content that links to a page, make sure the site is appropriate. You will not be rewarded for coaxing a visitor to a site that is unrelated to the content they read just (or have been watched depending on the content you provided).

12. Don't forget your roots, be respectful. It's easy for your head to become famous.

When you become the bright star on your market, please see who helped you get to the front of the pack. (This ties a little in #7) 13. Don't be scared to try new stuff, stay fresh.

Everyone on the internet knows how fast things are changing. Keep up with new media content, new website styles, and new market interests.

You will keep top ratings by keeping up with new data.

Developing a plan for Social Media Optimization Social Media has multiple purposes.

You need to define your intent, and then publish content to promote it. Social Media Optimization includes marketing, visibility, charity, traffic creation, awareness increasing, sales increase, credibility, etc. Make sure you build content that you publish and create for this purpose.

15. Wisely choose your SMO tactics.

Only about 10 percent of the content available on the web is a content creator. The remaining 90% are users and are prepared to share their content. Make it easy to absorb and distribute your content. Make sure you create content that will have the most significant effect on your original purpose (which could be advertising, reputation, charity, traffic increase, build popularity, sales increase, credibility, etc.).

16. Make the optimization of the social media-SMO part of your process and best practices.

We all know that each website must include different search engine optimization tactics.

Just like keywords and phrases in your title tags, you can find ways to incorporate elements of the automation of social media in designing your website. These may involve small details such as adding social bookmark tags on your page or promote incoming links to the "linked recently" list I have covered in #3.

17. Don't be afraid to let go and let others own a text or idea.

Finally, you don't be afraid to let others run with it when you create a trend, spark an idea, or develop a new subject. Collaboration is essential. Others can boost the original design and thank you for the beginning.

CPSIA information can be obtained
at www.ICGtesting.com
Printed in the USA
BVHW091236040521
606415BV00004B/964